Carolyn Westbrook

A ROMANCE
WITH
FRENCH LIVING

Carolyn Westbrook

A ROMANCE
WITH
FRENCH LIVING

Interiors inspired by classic French style

Photography by Keith Scott Morton and Eric Richards

CICO BOOKS
LONDON NEW YORK

Published in 2014 by CICO Books
an imprint of Ryland Peters & Small Ltd
519 Broadway, 5th Floor, New York, NY 10012
20–21 Jockey's Fields, London WC1R 4BW

www.rylandpeters.com

10 9 8 7 6 5 4 3 2 1

To Jacquelyn
What started out as business, with you as one of my best
customers, has become a true friendship. I appreciate
everything you do to make my books more wonderful.
Much love to you and Steve.
xo,
Carolyn

A CIP catalog record for this book is available from the
Library of Congress and the British Library.

ISBN 978 1 78249 138 5

Printed in China

Photographs: Keith Scott Morton and Eric Richards
Design: Carole Ash
Copy editor: Helen Ridge

Contents

Introduction

above and opposite: TWO DIFFERENT EXAMPLES OF MY TAKE ON FRENCH STYLE. BOTH TYPES OF CHAIR ARE SOPHISTICATED AND ELEGANT, YET ALSO COMFORTABLE.

above: THE VARIOUS ELEMENTS IN THIS BATHROOM COMBINE TO CREATE A SPACE THAT IS FUNCTIONAL BUT ALSO VERY ROMANTIC.

DECORATING IS MY PASSION but I've never been one to follow the latest styles and trends, preferring to stick to the classics. I fell in love with French style long before I ever set foot in Paris, and over the years it has become an important part of my own decorating style. Many say that my style is romantic, and I would agree, although I am not sure you can pigeonhole my many looks into just one style. I like a relaxed, comfortable home, not one that is pretentious or stuffy. And I adore the country life, where beauty happens right before your very eyes.

My decorating is not limited to interiors. I love parties and creating just the right décor and atmosphere for them. I also love to cook. I am from the South and, when it comes to hospitality, I have tried to take over where my grandparents left off. They lived on a farm, and I remember my grandfather dressed in overalls, chewing on his cigar. But there was always a smile on his face, too. He loved people, and enjoyed sitting down and breaking bread with anyone who happened to stop by. My grandmother would always have a pot of beans on the stove and a pan of cornbread in the oven. She could make a meal stretch from four people to ten people as fast as she could whip up some homemade biscuits.

As a tribute to them and their way of life, I really wanted this book to celebrate the gatherings with family and friends that each of us should be enjoying. We are all so caught up with work and appointments and school and whatever that we forget how important it is to laugh and have fun together. My daughter was married this year, and when my aunt and my cousins, some of whom I hadn't seen in years, showed up at the wedding, I was reminded of the fact. In light of that, part of this book is dedicated to the romance of a wedding and the fun of a family party. I hope you will love this book and look at it over and over again. Enjoy!

xoxo Carolyn

PART ONE

French-Inspired Interiors

A COTTAGE IN THE COUNTRY • URBAN FARMHOUSE
ESSENTIALLY FRENCH • IN THE GARDEN

CHAPTER 1

A Cottage in the Country

MANY PEOPLE SPEND THEIR LIVES DREAMING OF A COTTAGE IN THE COUNTRY. FOR SOME, THIS IS NO more than a weekend retreat, while for others it is a full-time dream come true. This is where one comes to get away from the grind of the city, with its ringing phones and deadlines. As you near your destination, the roads turn to tracks, and the gravel crackles under the tires. You can picture the woods surrounding the cottage and its huge garden colored with brilliant sunflowers.

WHEN THE COTTAGE COMES INTO VIEW, you find you can breathe more easily and stress seems to simply melt away. This is where you can hear yourself think, where you can walk barefoot in the grass; where you can stay up late gazing at the stars, then sleep under an antique quilt. With the windows flung wide open, you can smell the country air as you drift away into your dreams.

One can dream of the beauty and potential in this old, neglected farmhouse, set deep in the countryside. The two ornate "P" initials in the metalwork of the outer doors remind me of similar doors in New York City, and give a sense of the building's former grandeur. It takes a brave soul to undertake such a renovation. It is not for the faint of heart or for someone who lacks the passion and the vision of what this house can be.

This farmhouse is primed for the renovation that awaits it, and the homeowner has already dreamed of the romantic dinner parties that will once again take place there, with the dining table surrounded with urns of decadent roses and glowing candles.

AN ornate French armchair adds a sophisticated touch to a rather neglected farmhouse that is just waiting to be reborn.

This country home is stunning, and its design and decoration were well thought out. To me, it feels like an old-world home sitting deep in the French countryside. The structure is made from stone and old wooden beams and ceiling boards, in their original colors. A glass room on the back of the house allows one to see all the nature just outside. A baby grand piano makes this room all the more imposing and is perfectly in keeping with the décor. I am an advocate of using elaborate décor and furnishings even in small homes, to make them seem larger and more dramatic. A cottage is more like a palace with old painted wall murals, large and breathtaking furnishings, and antique oil paintings with just the right patina.

HIGH-BACKED WING CHAIRS FLANK AN ANTIQUE CHEST, CREATING A COZY NOOK FOR CONVERSATION.

A PRIMITIVE INTERIOR IS COMPLETELY TRANSFORMED BY ELEGANT FRENCH-
STYLE FURNITURE AND FURNISHINGS. OVERLEAF YOU CAN SEE THE OTHER
END OF THIS STUNNING ROOM, WITH VIEWS TO THE GARDEN BEYOND.

gorgeous paintings,
along with plenty of SEATING,
make for a *beautiful* and
comfortable HOME

The country-house style is one that I have written about before, but my excuse is that it is one of my absolute favorites. As you can see on the previous spread, the style can be quite stately, with a baby grand piano and a spectacular, perfectly aged, painted mural. Yet this space is also welcoming, whether for a brief visit or to gather around the piano at a special party.

The paneled ceilings in this farmhouse have been meticulously rendered. Together with the massive exposed wooden beams, they bring enormous warmth and intimacy to a large area. Venetian mirrors and gorgeous paintings, along with plenty of seating, also contribute to making this into a beautiful and comfortable home.

Taking center stage as guests enter the house is the dining room, which forms part of the overall living area.

With plenty of space to maneuver, it is a quick and easy task to add leaves to the table, if needed, to cater for a bigger party. For such occasions, an antique metal wine rack, resting against the wall, is capable of handling an impressive number of bottles.

Offering a focal point at one end of the room are two gorgeous upholstered high-backed chairs, which flank an antique wooden chest. This spot is masterfully styled, with a large antique Venetian mirror hanging on the wall, and a beautiful orchid protruding from an antique pewter vessel.

Along the side wall sits a trestle table with two antique sconces hanging over it, lighting the huge unframed print of a farm scene. Two decorative French armchairs stand either side of the table, and a stool covered in an antique zebra rug completes the look.

FRESH tomatoes, basil, *and* lettuces are
gathered in
the YARD *and* brought
in for tonight's DINNER

Everyone loves to gather in a kitchen, and the one featured above is definitely French-inspired—the resident is a real chef and even grates the "sel" from a stone to go on top of, and in, her favorite dishes. For her, a commercial cooktop is essential, but although the hardware here leans toward the modern, the kitchen has the feel of home. Cooking utensils are conveniently stored in urns alongside the stove. Plenty of storage is provided in the fitted cabinets, which are painted a wonderful shade of earthy gray. The open shelving also provides easily accessible storage, as well as space to show off treasured pieces of ironstone. With a small table close by, the chef can easily cook and converse with guests at the same time. The gardens outside seem to go on forever, providing the freshest vegetables and herbs.

A porch is an important feature of any country house, and this one does not disappoint. Decorated with plenty of urns filled with plants, statuary, and even a small wagon, it is a welcoming sight for all those who enter this country paradise, whether visitor or resident. An old-fashioned bell over the door happily announces the latest arrivals. On warm evenings, a large wooden bench with cushions begs to be sat on.

Inside, overlooking the porch, is a pair of antique chairs, standing either side of a distressed pedestal table. With the fabulous lamp above, mounted on a stone bracket, this is the perfect setting for gazing outside during inclement weather, with a glass of wine to hand.

Antique wooden beams were used in the construction of
this French-inspired country house, and make appealing
divisions between different areas. The homeowner has a
passion for entertaining, and plenty of seating is provided
for guests, from dining chairs to a sleek, curvaceous
couch with oversized cushions and upholstered
armchairs—linen abounds in this marvelous space
made for gatherings. Appropriately, the house comes
complete with a gorgeous French bulldog named Bogie.

The living room of this country cottage is an eclectic mix of styles, which I happen to adore. The industrial feel of the coffee table, made with a glass top and a base of antique metal oar blades, works incredibly well with the amazing modern art on the walls. Similarly, the tarnished, wall-mounted fire hood and electric lamp chandelier are bold but successful additions, as are the stone fountain and statue, brought inside from the yard. Sunflowers, picked in the neighboring field and displayed in a vintage fire bucket, create a vibrant splash of color. Continuing the eclectic theme, a modern, low-slung, slipcovered sofa appears perfectly at ease here.

white-paneled

WALLS and a NATURAL WOVEN floor *covering* make a fitting NEUTRAL backdrop to this *eclectic* mix of STYLES

This is another wonderfully done kitchen. The oven is a commercial beauty, and the Calcutta marble of the giant island gleams. I also happen to be in love with the antique leather-top bar stools that surround it. Anything remotely unsightly is concealed or "built in"—there is a drawer for the microwave, and the refrigerator looks like custom-made cabinetry—while open shelving serves as both decorative display and functional storage for attractive china, glasses, and vases. Old boards make up the butcher-block countertops, which warm up the white cabinets. This is a kitchen that most people would dream of.

GROWING JUST OUTSIDE THE BACK DOOR ARE SUNFLOWERS, WHICH ARE CUT AND BROUGHT INSIDE FOR THE ULTIMATE FARM KITCHEN ARRANGEMENT. JUST VISIBLE BEHIND THEM ARE THE ORNATE METAL BRACKETS USED TO SUPPORT THE SHELVES.

A METAL CAKE STAND GIVES HEIGHT TO A PRETTY DISPLAY OF HERBS AND BERRIES IN VINTAGE POTTERY JARS THAT ONCE HELD PASTES AND JAM.

Judging by the contents of this bar room, it comes as no surprise to learn that the owner is something of a wine connoisseur. Standing on top of an old wooden barrel is an enormous and eye-catching "tree" wine rack, for holding some of his extensive wine collection. Vintage wine crates contain masterfully painted antique wine jugs and also serve as side tables, while the walls hold shelving containing the finest bottles that money can buy.

Sampling the wines is an absolute joy in the antique leather, hooded chairs, which were designed originally to be used in front of a fireplace and keep the heat in. They are a beautiful addition to this thoughtfully designed space, which looks as though it is straight out

of a baronial castle in Europe. Farmhouse style can vary, and this bar room, which is really more of a wine room, does represent a somewhat sophisticated version. The farmhouse to which it belongs is, without doubt, all about cooking and entertaining.

On the opposite wall is the actual bar. Concealed ingeniously within antique cabinetry are a sink, a refrigerator, and storage. The cabinets are one of a kind and offer unique, intricate carvings and a patina that benefit this room enormously. Built in, they look as though they have been a feature for many, many years. The old bottles and crates displayed on the top cabinet add to the sophisticated ambience of the room.

One thing I find so great about country homes is that they often come with an outbuilding, like a barn or a tractor shed, which can be transformed into a guest cottage. Many such structures have metal roofs, which I'm particularly fond of—when raindrops patter down on them, the atmosphere inside becomes even cozier.

This quaint little building, once a barn, now has a dual role as a place for entertaining downstairs with guest accommodation above. The owner decided to "go green" when renovating, incorporating recycled and reused wooden boards, vintage lighting, and extraordinary antique accessories. Old windows have also been added, along with a crusty mirror and a wonderful antique wooden chandelier. There is even a banquette constructed from planks of recycled wood. All these discarded pieces have been given a new lease of life and are allowed to thrive once more.

In the corner nook nearby (see right), the centerpiece is a fabulous French sofa, but the rest of the décor has a more primitive air, such as the simple painting of a bird hanging above a galvanized water container planted with greenery. Internal windows allow you to see into the other rooms.

ALL THE
elements used to REMODEL
the BARN have been *recycled*
and given a new life

CHAPTER 2

Urban Farmhouse

Urban farmhouse is sort of an oxymoron, but the houses featured in this chapter seem to dictate the title. In these homes, you really get the best of both worlds. As you all know, I am very familiar with ultra-modern, urban surroundings, having grown up with them. The living spaces here are also urban and their interiors sleek. But the important difference is that as well as being high on style, they are warm too. They tell a story, and that is their real genius.

I HAPPEN TO *love* THE FACT
that we *resurrect* things that H A V E
been *discarded* or S O L D A S *junk,*
A N D T H E N let them come *alive*
again in just the *right* E N V I R O N M E N T

IN THE URBAN FARMHOUSE, primitive objects are used in a clean and modern way that makes you look at them differently. Wood plays an integral part, used for windows, walls, ceilings, and beams that support the structures. The ceilings in many of these houses are artworks in themselves, with beaded board in varying shades showing off overhead. Some feature natural wood-colored walls, while others have been whitewashed. Farm implements are used for industrial-style light fixtures for a unique effect.

Recycling plays an important part in the work of any antiques buyer or designer. I happen to love the fact that we resurrect things that have been discarded or sold as junk, and then let them come alive again in just the right environment. It just doesn't get any better than that.

Being green is so "in" at the moment, but my mother showed me the ropes of how to spot the best stuff and recycle it in our family homes for years. It is important to realize that new items have no story, no charm, no patina. Put simply, they are boring, not to mention disposable. Now, it is up to my children and their counterparts to carry on the generational treasure hunt and ensure that they hold on to what's worth keeping.

In each of these homes, there is a collision of styles, but it is masterfully done. In the living area shown opposite, it is hard to say what one should look at first. The massive whitewashed fireplace begs to be seen, but it is not to be outdone by the overhead industrial light fixture, which has been recycled. One can even see some sort of gauge or dial at the top. It really is an amazing piece. Something as simple as old wooden screens serve as artwork over the fireplace, while an antique trunk, showing its age, is the perfect choice as a coffee table. With all the antique and recycled parts and pieces picked up along the way and over time, this room has come together wonderfully.

The styling of this staircase leading up from the living space would not be out of place in a New York or Paris loft. The numbered stairs greet you as you come in through the door. It is such a simple decorating choice and yet so smart.

The black on the stairs sets off the white numbers and the surrounding white walls, creating a sense of drama in the room. The old lighted sign, complementing the wooden beam, points the way up the staircase, and is a delightfully whimsical touch. The couch is simply slipcovered for ease and convenience, while grain-sack pillows are the perfect couch cushions.

For all of us who have looked at a blank space or a nook and then thought, hmm, what should I do here, this could be the answer. The shelving at the top of the stairs was custom-made to fit each antique trunk and suitcase. Made of leather, metal, or really heavy pasteboard, and sporting different styles of handle and hardware, the pieces of luggage, with a history all of their own, form an original piece of art as well as useful storage.

A large farmhouse sink and beaded board speak of a farmhouse, while the industrial-style light fixtures above have been fashioned from ordinary antique chicken feeders. Chunky wooden shelves on metal brackets make practical and attractive storage for the ironstone dishes.

In the dining area, a long whitewashed harvest table is ready to seat the many guests that stop by this convivial home, with an old bench offering seating on one side. The table centerpiece is a collection of trophy cups, wicker bottles and baskets, and leather-bound books. An antique birdhouse, displayed at the window, has been recycled as artwork.

The living room featured overleaf is truly meant for living. Tossed over the sofa is a vintage white blanket, to serve as a relaxed slipcover, with random red ticking pillows creating colorful contrasts, along with the red ticking wing chair, which fits delightfully into the mix. Serious-looking faces peer from antique paintings and prints, while chrome elements come into play, making this an interior that feels altogether very well done.

the NATURAL
beauty of the WOODEN WALLS
makes a *stunning* contrast with
the WHITE BATHROOM

Stripping away the wallpaper in this bedroom (left) revealed the most beautiful wooden walls. Instead of then covering them with Sheetrock, which, sadly, many people would do, the owners celebrated their natural beauty and age. The wood makes a stunning contrast to the stark white of the bathroom glimpsed through the dividing drapes. French sconces hang from the wall and a stack of white towels in a basket make one long for a soak in the tub.

The bathroom opposite is similarly decked out in white but with touches of color and a wooden floor to soften the look. The pane of glass in the unusual antique door is surrounded by smaller squares of colored glass, like a picture frame, creating a piece of art. The engraved panel below echoes the bow-fronted, French-style vanity. The homeowners have surrounded themselves with a door that is part of the history of a dear friend and tells his story—the door was brought from an orphanage, where this friend lived as a child. The door is not only beautiful but has meaning as well.

CHAPTER 3

Essentially French

IT IS MY THOUGHT THAT FRENCH STYLE JUST SEEMS TO ADD AN ELEMENT OF SOPHISTICATION TO ANY home. If you study the look for just a moment, you can see that it is all about the details and achieving the right mix. Wherever the homes featured here happen to be, the interiors possess some of that French style that we all crave. Notice that even though they are rather sophisticated, they are far from being cold and unwelcoming. On the contrary, they are warm and inviting, which is what makes a beautiful home.

IT IS THE *attention* to *detail* that UNDERLIES the *success* of the DÉCOR

THE GRACEFUL, WINDING STAIRCASE, anchored to the floor by a baby grand piano, forms the structural basis for this entryway. It makes a breathtaking welcome to the house but it is the attention to detail, seen in the beautifully detailed moldings and intricately carved spindles of the balustrade, that underlies the success of the décor.

Lighting is very important to any room, and here it has been carefully thought out. A skylight at the top of the stairs bathes the entrance in natural light, which is supplemented by wall sconces and a large lantern hanging down low from a curlicue grille. Dimmers have been added to the light switches, so that the right ambience can be created, whatever the time of day.

Like the skylight grille, this display table (right) is another example of fine metalwork. The classical-style sculpture and exotic shells and coral coordinate well with one another and are displayed to perfection against the black tabletop. The fleurs-de-lis featured in the curvaceous table legs are a subtle homage to France.

The nook next to the fireplace is perfectly appointed. An antique black chest is a romantic piece, with its painted garlands of flowers and curvaceous shape. Hanging from a drawer handle is a silk tassel, a whimsical but also effective decorative detail. The tall lamp on top, also an antique, mimics the colors of the chest and casts a subtle glow, together with the gleaming crystal rose bowls filled with flickering candles. In the same color tones as the chest and lamp is a gothic-shaped mirror in a carved wooden frame. Reflected in its glass is an interesting collection of oil paintings on the other side of the room.

Just past the nook is a hallway beautifully tiled in different-colored diamond shapes between the chair rail and baseboard. The two wall sconces cast a romantic glow on the painting hanging between them. This piece has been passed down the homeowner's family, which makes it all the more special. Surrounding oneself with objects that have meaning is particularly important and brings to mind favored memories.

The bar manages to look both modern and vintage at the same time, and is absolutely breathtaking. From the distressed silver reflective tiles used for the backsplash to the amazing hammered-metal bar sink, this space has been very well thought out for maximum appeal. Adding to the distinction, sparkle, and beauty are vintage silver trays for serving champagne or snacks, and a bar towel picked up at a Parisian boutique.

The open fireplace is a decorative as well as practical addition to the massive living room. Hanging above the mantelpiece is a painting of a summer garden, which blends beautifully with the color of the wall and introduces an element of romance. In hues of honey-gold, the antique books also echo the paint color and the artwork. Sandwiched between objects of varying heights and sizes, the books form part of a harmonious display.

ADDING TO THE *distinction*, *sparkle*, and BEAUTY are *vintage* SILVER TRAYS for serving champagne or *snacks*

The same golden tones are also found in this beautiful dining area. In summer, the French doors are flung wide open to allow in the breeze, which flutters the gorgeous silk drapes, and the sound of water bubbling in the fountain can be heard as the family dines. Blooms of hydrangeas spilling from glass containers give an energizing dash of white.

The seating in the room shown above is altogether sumptuous, and the golden hues throughout bring a warmth and intimacy to the space. A rich variety of fabrics has been used to upholster the sofa, ottoman, chairs, and pillows, but they have all been carefully selected so that the overall effect is harmonious and easy on the eye.

THE VERY HIGH
CEILING OF THIS
GOTHIC-STYLE
ROOM ALLOWS FOR
A SECOND LEVEL
OF WINDOWS AND
AN UNUSUAL
INTERNAL BALCONY.

The soft golden tones in the living room are made dramatic with the contrasting black metals and dark wood trims, windows, and doors that have been added to the mix. The arched French doors, leading out to the yard, and those opening from the balcony above have been trimmed in dark wood, while hanging from the lofty ceiling is a spectacular, dark iron chandelier. The brick detail surrounding the doorway, which leads into the kitchen and keeping room, also contributes to the overall interest. With plenty of seating, this characterful room is a magnet for guests.

The kitchen (right) just around the corner is the epitome of French style. Above the glass, the door is carved with the words "Garde-Manger," which means "Keeper of the Food" in English. It makes the perfect pantry door.

the KITCHEN
is the *epitome* of
french
style

Just outside the bar and just inside the French doors is this wonderful spot in which to sit and enjoy a glass of wine. It contains an unexpected but wholly successful mix of styles, from the rustic stone walls and animal-skin rug, through an industrial-looking metal table, to the classically French armchairs with French script on their backs. The carved detailing of swags and bows on the wood of the chairs is exquisitely done, then gilded for the perfect finish. The classical-style bust, refashioned into a modern work of art, perches on top of its own intricately carved plinth.

IN THIS
well-executed bath,
where S P A C E is not an *issue,*
the E L E G A N T, claw-foot tub
is *able* to take
C E N T E R stage

Bathing in an uncluttered bathroom with no distractions
is the quickest way to unwind at the end of a busy day.
In this well-executed bath, where space is not an issue,
the elegant, claw-foot tub is able to take center stage,
accompanied by a vintage slipper chair in delicate white
slipcovers. The internal glass window offers a view into
the large tiled shower Beneath it is an antique heating
grate. Although the blind at the other window provides
all the privacy required, pretty lace drapes, held back
either side by metal bosses, soften the hard lines and
introduce a feminine quality.

A WALL
of mirrors SHOWS OFF
the beautiful *reflection*
OF THE BEDROOM just
beyond the door

French cabinetry brings style and sophistication to this contemporary, white-painted bathroom. A gorgeous piece of furniture, warmed by the dark wood floor and the natural stone sink, it is nevertheless kept modern by the clean-lined fixtures. A wall of mirrors above reflects light from the bedroom beyond.

Just because a kitchen is the most practical room in the house, there is no reason why it can't also be made to look pretty. Hanging at this kitchen window, made special with antique lace curtain panels, is an extraordinary petite chandelier. When the sun catches the large, chunky, antique prisms, it adds a touch of sparkle to the room.

CHAPTER 4

In the Garden

THE GARDEN IS WHERE YOU WILL OFTEN FIND ME, NO MATTER THE TIME OF YEAR. "IN THE GARDEN" is one of my all-time favorite church hymns, and the garden is the best place to commune with nature, to think, and to pray. It just makes me feel better to plunge my hands into the earth, and to plant a seed and watch it grow is exciting and gratifying. In this chapter, we have all sorts of gardens—vegetable, flower, and herb—some with fruit trees laden with fruit, and bees buzzing about them.

AT OUR PLANTATION, flowers grow randomly, mixed in a collage of color and kind. Marigolds are planted at the edge of a garden to deter pests. Vegetables are picked at the peak of flavor and color for tonight's dinner. The tractor is brought out to plow up the earth, while our rooster, The Colonel, watches all the goings-on.

What a treat it is to have your own garden. Eating the best of fresh vegetables and herbs, knowing exactly where they came from, is the ultimate in healthy living. Here, there is no wax on the vegetables and no genetically modified food. The eggs come directly from the hens themselves, with their clucking announcing a new egg, and they reluctantly step away to let you gather it. Cucumbers are picked for salads and for canning pickles. Tomatoes are plucked for fresh salsa, and a random bouquet of flowers and rosemary can become the centerpiece for a kitchen table.

When I was a child, one of my mother's best friends was an amazing designer. I remember that she had a plate-glass window looking out over a water garden. This was completely covered with an overhead trellis draped in vines. There was a gorgeous aged fountain statue, of a woman with an urn. Water poured out of it and back down into the pool, which was surrounded by lush plant life and waterlilies. I could have stood for hours at the window, looking at the pond and its bright orange fish. I really wanted to get into the water and touch them. It was something of a mirage but I always thought that, someday, I would have a water garden like that myself.

The gardens featured here vary from inside spaces to outdoor water gardens, complete with brightly colored goldfish. It is the water element in the outdoor patio garden that makes it so special.

The gorgeous water garden overleaf boasts architecture that reminds me of a courtyard in New Orleans or France. Later in the chapter, we feature a French garden house. It is actually a cooking school but, with the farm doors thrown open, it becomes an open-air garden house where the roosters roam at will.

A fountain is an easy way of adding beauty to your yard, and the sound of water trickling is incredibly soothing. Don't forget to furnish your porches, too. That way, you have a comfortable place to sit or rock, as you enjoy your gardens, regardless of the weather.

Blue and white is a classic color combination and always makes a statement, as shown on page 61. Here, a menagerie of blue and white pottery in all shapes and sizes dresses up a garden space beautifully. Having only white flowers and green foliage ensures that nothing detracts from their impact.

If you have always dreamed of a garden, then get your hands dirty—it's not rocket science, and there is so much information online. Of course, there is always trial and error, too. The important thing is just to dig in.

WHEN FILLED WITH VARIOUS FORMS OF PLANT LIFE, STATUARY, URNS, AND CANDLELIGHT, AN ORDINARY GARDEN SPACE BECOMES VISUALLY STUNNING.

WITH ITS LUSH PLANTING AND DRAMATIC ARCHITECTURE, THIS BACKYARD COMES AS A DELIGHTFUL

SURPRISE. A REMARKABLE PLACE FOR ENTERTAINING, IT HAS BUILT-IN GRILLS, BAR REFRIGERATORS,

ICE MACHINES, AND, MOST IMPORTANT, PLENTY OF SEATING—THE KEY TO ANY SUCCESSFUL

ENTERTAINING SPACE. THE IVY-CLAD ARCHES ARE REMINISCENT OF COURTYARDS IN NEW ORLEANS

OR PARIS. CHANNELS OF WATER, FILLED WITH FISH, TO THE GUESTS' DELIGHT, SURROUND THE PATIO.

OVERLEAF, THE SOUND OF WATER TRICKLING FROM THE ORNATE FAUCETS SOOTHES THE SOUL.

sunflowers climb
their way TOWARD the SUN
with the *help* of a
charming GARDEN TRIPOD
made of WOOD

This corner of a country garden (seen opposite), shown at the height of summer, is at its finest. Sunflowers climb their way toward the sun with the help of a charming garden tripod made of wood. Accompanied by plumbago, basil, peppers, and rosemary, the setting is full of joyous color and tantalizing scents. A terra-cotta statue of a rooster adds to the farmhouse appeal.

The heart of the countryside is the perfect spot for an aviary (right). This unique design was built by my friend Ludmil, who is something of an expert at creating bespoke aviaries. It is a grand home for these beautiful doves, which are enjoyed by everyone who visits.

For me, a sunroom—or garden room—
is a magical place, especially when there
are plants everywhere and it feels like an
indoor garden oasis. Displaying garden
statuary simply adds to the atmosphere.

This table has been set to hold
everything needed for an evening dinner
party taking place in the gardens.
Although the guests will spend most of
their time outdoors, the buffet will be
kept in the garden room, safe from the
elements. Even so, it has been decked out
beautifully. A magnificent cheese plant in
a wicker basket is complemented by the
garden urn of cyclamen and orchids on
the table, their vivid petals matching the
strong color of the tablecloth. Flickering
candlelight provides a romantic glow,
while a table lamp lights up the far corner
of the room.

THE PERFECT SHADE OF PLUM IN
THE TABLECLOTH AND TRANSFERWARE
DISHES IS REFLECTED IN THE CYCLAMEN
AND ORCHIDS DISPLAYED IN THE URN.

I am
always on the H U N T for
transferware,
which is a *great*
C O L L E C T I B L E

I am always on the hunt for transferware, which is a great collectible and comes in a number of different colors. The plum-colored harvest scenes of these dishes are probably my favorite, and they look striking with the magenta silk tablecloth that covers the serving table on this occasion. A skirted corner table makes a beautiful statement, with a soft halo of light from the lamp and a purple hydrangea potted up in an ornate ironstone container. Once again, candlelight abounds.

Whenever I visit Paris, I always make sure that I peruse the city's fabric shops. Many of these can be found close to the Basilica of the Sacré-Coeur, which is a landmark historic church. On one trip, while walking the streets, I happened to come across an unbelievable plum-colored toile peeking from a store window. Immediately, I could visualize it paired with my plum transferware dishes. Panels of this toile now hang from my garden-room windows to marvelous effect.

Set in the middle of a rambling country garden, this rustic space is a cooking school, where one can be educated in the delights of French cuisine. It also makes an atmospheric venue for casual dinner parties and wine tastings.

From the ceiling made up of rough planks of wood to the fabulous primitive tile-top table—the center of attention—everything about the space is utterly charming. And with the blue and white tablecloths and napkins, it exudes the French atmosphere that is so intoxicating and wonderful.

THE ROOSTERS DON'T LIKE TO MISS OUT ON THE FINE DINING. WHEN THE DOORS ARE FLUNG OPEN, THEY CANNOT RESIST TAKING A PEEK INSIDE.

PART TWO

It's All in the Detail

WHITE LINEN • WORLD TRAVELER

A LOVE OF BOOKS

CHAPTER FIVE

White Linen

FOR ME, WHITE LINEN CONJURES UP THOUGHTS
of crisp white sheets and luxurious bedding, beautiful
curtains, comfy couches, snow-white tablecloths, napkins,
and sprinklings of the fragrant white body powder with the same
name. I have always adored linen, and when it is white, it serves as
a base and does not compete with other elements in the room.

I LOVE TO THROW A MONOGRAMMED linen bed sheet over a table to make a grand tablecloth. As I roam through flea markets in France, I am always on the hunt for vintage monogrammed French linen sheets. The monograms embroidered many years ago are exquisite. They are all different, varying in font and size, and sometimes the color of the thread, but all extraordinary. Of course, most of the monograms you will find will not match your own, but it is more about the look of them than the actual initial.

Linen is a natural, organic fiber that breathes and offers amazing comfort in clothing and bedding. Here we used a neutral palette of oatmeal and white, colors that blend with the glorious antique rug that I picked up on my travels. It had been stored in a warehouse for some time, waiting to make a showing here in our home. For me, it's always about the mix, and some of the items that I love are always with me, just reinvented in different vignettes.

I am constantly recreating my environment, to keep everything looking fresh. It is very easy to do with basic pieces in neutral colors, such as sofas and chairs, while a dining space can be changed completely with something as simple as a tablecloth. Made of linen, it will soften the look of a room, and different colors can be used as the seasons change. Similarly, a rug against a neutral base can completely transform a space.

THIS DINING ROOM OFFERS A SUBTLE, ETHEREAL BEAUTY AS THE SUN BEAMS THROUGH THE WHITE LINEN DRAPES. CANDLES ON THE TABLE KEEP THE SETTING INTIMATE.

left: LUSCIOUS PINK CABBAGE ROSES AND PINK BERRIES, DRAPING OVER THE LIP OF THE VINTAGE GARDEN URN, ARE THE CENTERPIECE OF THIS TABLE SETTING. THE SOFT GLOW OF CANDLELIGHT ENHANCES THE VARIOUS ELEMENTS, MAKING THE TABLE EVEN MORE INVITING.

---

right: I HAPPEN TO LOVE THESE WICKER WINE BOTTLES, AND HAVE A LARGE COLLECTION IN VARIOUS SIZES. AGAINST THE SMOOTHNESS OF THE GLASSES AND DECANTER, THE TEXTURE THAT THEY ADD TO THE TABLETOP IS SOMETHING I CANNOT GET ENOUGH OF.

---

far right: THE GOURMET CHEESES, COVERED WITH VINTAGE GLASS CLOCHES TO KEEP THEM FROM DRYING OUT, ARE THE FOCUS OF THIS APPETIZING VIGNETTE. TOGETHER WITH THE BASES—AN ORNATE SILVER PLATTER AND ANTIQUE WOODEN BREADBOARD—THEY MAKE FOR AN EVEN MORE INTERESTING TABLE.

This table setting is a fine example of what layering is all about. From a vintage garden urn filled with gorgeous cabbage roses and topped with an aged statue of a cherub, to antique wooden breadboards, to my favored Ironstone and spooners, everything comes together for an inspired result.

Speaking of inspired results, let us remind ourselves of the beauty of candlelight, which can transform a dining table with its soft, romantic glow and make any party more special and intimate. Table lamps in discreet corners help preserve the desired atmosphere, something that is impossible with overhead lighting.

Make sure that you have plenty of chairs available for your guests, but keep in mind that they do not have to be positioned around the table all the time. They can act as beautiful décor in their own right and then be brought in around the table as and when they are needed.

Repurposing objects is the key to any good interior, and this tabletop is no different. A mint julep cup has become a spooner. I always speak of my love for "spooners," and many have questioned what they are. The answer is: a traditional holder for spoons, usually a tall glass vessel, often set on a pedestal, like a goblet. Practical and pretty on this tabletop, they are filled not only with spoons but also with a selection of knives and breadsticks. They are incredibly versatile and can even be used for flowers.

The way that things are plated and served is of particular importance. An antique pine chest is used here as a "buffet" for storage and serving. Carved wooden

breadboards can double up as chargers or, as seen here, as cutting boards and serving platters for delicious cheeses and crackers. A vintage red wine looks so much more appealing when poured into a gorgeous crystal decanter, which adds its own beauty to the table.

Being the good Southern girl that I am, there had to be a silver tray somewhere. Actually, there are stacks of them. I do love a silver tray, but I find that my love is reserved for those with just the right patina—they have to be a little tarnished. There also has to be a certain "weight" to them. Unlike antique trays, modern versions tend to be flimsy, offer no carvings, and simply don't have the same appeal. As well as being used for their original purpose of serving, silver trays are also the perfect surface for displaying collections.

When reinventing your interior for a special occasion, do not be limited in your thinking. If you have a fabulous piece of garden statuary in your yard, bring it inside. That goes for flowers, blooming branches, and greenery, too. These can make fabulous seasonal arrangements. I am famous for going out on nature walks with my clippers and coming back with rosemary, cedar branches, and berries in the winter, sunflowers in the fall, and who knows what in the spring—it can range from pear-tree limbs that are blossoming to hydrangeas and mint—to use in a table display. I guess I inherited this passion from my grandmother. She was always picking flowers for a bouquet in the house. Sometimes it was as simple as Indian paintbrushes and marigolds or the bright purple berries of a beauty bush.

For me,
PINE is a classic
and I have *always* LIKED
to SEE it in
my home

I have had this antique pine chest for a long time, although it was previously in another room. But, in the spirit of freshening things up, I moved it here. For me, pine is a classic and I have always liked to see it in my home. In this setting, its warmth is enhanced by the oatmeal-colored drapes, which divide the oversized space. Using drapes in this way as a partition, holding them in place with a tieback, helps to break a large room up and make it more inviting. The lamp on top of the chest, with its white linen shade, imparts an atmospheric glow to the oil painting, the urn of hydrangeas, and the bowl of pears. With the wicker-seat French chair alongside, this vignette could not be more beautiful.

I bought the gorgeous old painting of bluebirds and pears at a flea market. It has aged extremely well and has the perfect patina. The pears in the ironstone bowl were plucked from the pear trees in our backyard. I do love to decorate with fruit tree limbs, leaves, and fruit, and here I have draped a branch of leaves over the top. Here, the leaves and beautiful fruit are the decoration for this bowl and reflect the pear limbs in the painting behind.

top and above: **WHETHER USED PURELY FOR DECORATION OR TO EMBELLISH A PRACTICAL DISPLAY, I LOVE TO SEE MY FAVORED ORNAMENTS OF FARM ANIMALS SCATTERED AROUND THE HOUSE.**

As well as being the support for a much-needed lamp, the round table in the corner of the dining room is the setting for an interesting collection of objects that I happen to favor. You know that my mantra has always been to surround yourself with the things that you love. This way of thinking is what makes your home you. Here we have my favored wicker decanters, along with a small stack of antique leather-bound books… there really is nothing quite like them. Just out of the shot is a small framed photograph of my beloved Princess, who has passed, and Teddy, who is still with us. Princess was my plus-size schnauzer—no other dog will ever compare to her—so this picture is of one of my loves.

Photographs are an important part of making a home, and you should always consider framing your memories, whether of places you have visited or people who are dear to you, so that you can enjoy them every day.

The pine chest in the dining room (opposite) has been with me for years. It was one of the first pieces that I ever bought, at an auction, when I was just nineteen years old. It offers great storage for napkins, silver, and so on. Alongside the rather special Florentine lamp on top is another stack of my treasured Ironstone platters in different sizes, ready for serving, as needed. Looking magnificent on top of them is a beautiful white porcelain cow (left), which I found at an antiques market. It makes me smile every time I reach for a platter.

I admit I do have a passion for farm animals—perhaps because I live on a farm—and have many of the miniature metal farm animals that I have collected scattered throughout the house, as part of various displays. The delightful little metal cow and cockerel (top left) were made in Germany more than one hundred years ago. I find the detailing on them quite incredible.

THIS FANTASTIC GARDEN ROOM POSSESSES AN EFFORTLESS BEAUTY. IT IS A GLORIOUS VISION IN

WHITE, BUT THERE IS NO DANGER OF IT BEING OVERWHELMING, THANKS TO THE WARM WOODEN

FLOOR AND THE CONCRETE-TOPPED PEDESTAL TABLE THAT ANCHORS THE SCHEME.

THE DIFFERENT STYLES OF FURNITURE AND THE SUBTLE DIFFERENCES IN THEIR SLIPCOVERS AND

PILLOWS KEEP THIS INTERIOR INTERESTING. THE TALL WINDOWS GIVE THE ILLUSION THAT THE

WHITE LINEN DÉCOR IS FLOWING INTO THE OUTDOORS.

THE ABSENCE OF COLOR
in *white linen* makes it *perfect*
for major FURNITURE pieces,
where it *serves* as a
NEUTRAL base

After all these years creating linen bedding and pillows, linen is still my passion. And I can honestly say that there really is nothing else quite like linen to work with and have in your home. I always say, the more you wash it, the softer and better it gets. Slipcovers can be taken off and laundered the moment they get dirty and easily put back on, to sparkle once more.

The absence of color in white linen makes it perfect for major furniture pieces, where it serves as a neutral base and will not compete with other elements in the room. One can then bring in color and print through smaller things such as art, accessories, and pillows. That way, as you tire of a certain color or print, you can remove it much more easily and, usually, cheaply from the scheme and start over with your latest passion, still with the white furniture as your neutral base. Of course, there is nothing quite like an all-white palette, should you prefer an overall neutral look.

As well as being a big believer in keeping large furniture pieces in a neutral color, I think this should also apply to things that are difficult or expensive to change, such as bath and kitchen tiles and countertops. For these, it makes sense to stay away from trends and colors that will soon be ancient history—you don't want to end up with a backsplash, for example, that is out of date within a year.

The French-style armchair seen opposite is so inviting in its white tie-on slipcovers. When the weather is unkind, one simply has to sit here to feel as though one is outside.

Positioned just outside the French doors of the sunroom (opposite), this linen-covered table and wonderful chairs, upholstered in white and silver cowhide, would look equally at home inside the house. This is such a versatile spot, where one can entertain friends in the evening over an intimate dinner, enjoy cocktails, or even play a few games of cards. At night, pillar candles in their silver holders light up the space beautifully. Seated here during the day, one can watch the bunnies as they hop about the backyard.

THESE **wonderful** chairs are UPHOLSTERED in white *and* silver cowhide

Looking in the opposite direction, back into the house (left), the eye is greeted by a white tufted couch—yet another piece of gorgeous seating. On the coffee table in front and in a vintage glass aquarium, the homeowner, who spends as much time as possible at the ocean, has displayed a unique collection of coral and shells. Beyond, one glimpses the living and kitchen areas and an assortment of marvelous architectural elements, including an antique French urn, which is used as a humorous display surface for an old, classical-style bust made of concrete.

the FRENCH ARMOIRE is **beautifully** carved and **REFLECTS** the master bed in a *gorgeous* light

I am a big fan of the clothesline, which always reminds me of my childhood. My mom used to hang out the linen sheets to dry—a bed made up in white linen is like no other—and when she brought them in, they would smell wonderful. She would then put clean sheets on every bed, and sprinkle them with her favorite talcum powder. I still do that today.

My very manly seventeen-year old son, Nick, is, I admit, quite spoiled, and he still loves to come home to clean sheets and a powdered bed. I have managed to find a powder smelling of lavender and sage on sale in one of my friends' shops that is suitably masculine.

It begs one to relax, unwind, and be calm. It is not too fussy or overdone—just simple and elegant.

The French armoire opposite is beautifully carved and reflects the master bed in a gorgeous light. The light fixture, quite architectural in style, like an old lantern, fits the room perfectly. Decorating is very much like a puzzle, where you have to find the right elements to put together so that the finished result looks as though it is the way it was always intended. The whitewashed walls and gleaming hardwood floors provide just the right neutral backdrop. It is all very understated but very sophisticated at the same time.

This bath (opposite) adjoins the bedroom featured on the previous spread and is decorated in much the same way—very simply but with the finest pieces. A garden statue of a woman toweling off is an appropriate addition next to the tub. And what a tub this is—an antique that has been upgraded and introduced to the bath in all its splendor. The carved French corner chair is another fine piece for draping one's clothes.

The French chandelier glistens above, providing just the right romantic light for a late-night bubble bath. Fresh, clean, white towels are meticulously rolled and stored ready for use on the modern chrome and glass shelves, where white orchids contribute their sophisticated elegance. There is nothing better than a stack of white fluffy towels. Colors fade, and go in and out of fashion, but white is a classic. Not only that, but you can bleach white towels whenever you need to, in order to get them good and clean.

The photograph on the right shows another sleek, French-inspired bathroom. Complementing the pale aqua walls is a French-style chest, with peeling paint in a beautiful shade of gray. A modern tray on folding legs holds more beautiful orchids, as well as pretty containers for bath salts and delicate soaps. Antique wall sconces and a modern chrome chandelier provide the mixed lighting.

The French doors open onto a secluded patio, where one can sit at the outdoor table and enjoy a glass of wine before or after taking a bath. The patio is completely private, enclosed with walls of corrugated metal, and a fountain flows into a small basin against the wall. Plants growing in the ground and in pots provide welcome splashes of greenery.

CHAPTER 6

World Traveler

TRAVEL IS ONE OF THE BEST EDUCATIONS THAT LIFE HAS TO OFFER, AND NO ONE LOVES TO TRAVEL MORE than I. To learn about different cultures and different worlds is simply life-changing, and I am all about bringing something back with me as a permanent reminder of my experiences. The homes featured here all tell the stories of their owners —where they have been during the course of their lives, what they have seen, and what they simply cannot live without.

THE
eclectic mix of POSSESSIONS in
this ROOM *creates* an *inspired*
INTERIOR that is not soon forgotten

TRAVEL ALLOWS US to experience different cultures first-hand, and absorb a wide array of tastes and sounds. Inspiration can be found anywhere. When I visit New York, for example, I am always looking up—the architecture is amazing—but most people are looking down or straight ahead, and they are rushing, rushing, rushing. It is so important to slow down and enjoy the view. You never know what might inspire you.

As well as surrounding yourself with cherished memories of places visited and people met, it is also important to celebrate family heirlooms that have been passed down to you. Everyone's personal history will be different, which is what is so great about your own home. It should not look or smell or feel like anyone else's. That is why I am such an advocate of antiques versus mass-produced products from big-box retailers. It's funny, though, that big-box retailers send out their scouts to yard sales and antiques markets in search of treasures that they can reproduce. However, such reproductions are not the same thing as treasures that you find yourself, and they definitely do not possess the same patina that comes with age.

A close look at the skirted tabletop on page 99 reveals an assortment of treasures, displayed on an old wooden tray that was discovered while on a trip to England. Trays are perfect for displaying smaller items that you can pick up in your hand, to appreciate at close quarters. Here we have some small, silver-framed family portraits, a stack of favored books with wonderful leather covers, a magnifying glass, and a sands-of-time dispenser—not to mention the little tortoise-like antique box. I adore antique containers like this.

If you have small objects of interest that you adore, then think about displaying them on a tray or even on a coffee table. Such pieces are a great way to build an interior that reflects your personality, so that it becomes as beautiful, individual, and interesting as you are.

There really is nothing quite as dramatic and remarkable as the color blue, especially cobalt-blue, and in this room, it shows up in a stunning, modern way. The blue velvet drapes bring a touch of luxury and sophistication, as does the blue silk table skirt. This chimes in beautifully with the blue and white plant pot and the lamp shaped like a ginger jar.

The oversized brass and glass coffee table (see pages 100–1) adds a little contemporary touch, as does the chrome and glass bar cart. I have always had a passion for decanters of all shapes, sizes, and textures, and this bar cart is the perfect way to show them off. Fitted with casters, it can be easily moved to wherever it is needed.

Bar carts are all the rage right now in interior fashion. I have had this one for many years, and I decided it was

above: THE BLUE OF THE DRAPES AND TABLECLOTH IS PICKED OUT IN THE RUG AND GLASS VESSEL ON THE OVERSIZED BRASS AND GLASS COFFEE TABLE. THE REFLECTION IN THE MIRRORED PLANTER SERVES TO DOUBLE THE IMPACT.

left: ANTIQUE LIQUOR DECANTER BOTTLES——SOME CRYSTAL, SOME NOT——HAVE BEEN SCRUBBED CLEAN, FILLED, THEN HUDDLED TOGETHER ON A SILVER TRAY, TO CREATE THIS CHARMING DISPLAY. SET ON A BAR CART WITH CASTERS, THE DISPLAY IS ALSO VERY PRACTICAL.

the perfect space to display all the decanters that I have collected over the years. When I was young, my mother displayed decanters with colored water in shades of green and blue—maybe that is where my passion for these glass beauties started. I just love the detail on the glass and the way that they are all so different. Some are crystal, some are not… their monetary value really does not matter to me. As always, I buy what I love. The Asian screen that serves as the backdrop to the cart brings a further global elegance to the space.

Another rather special decanter is shown on the silver-etched tray on page 103. It is a ship's decanter, striking in appearance and quite ingenious in design. Made with a flat bottom and a low, bulbous shape, it will resist rolling about when the ship is out at sea. It is etched in

a beautiful script, which identifies it as the Captain's decanter. The mirrored top of the table reflects the pretty books and the other accoutrements of the space.

A collection of antique world globes—one was a piggy bank from the 1930s, given as a prize at a State Fair—in a variety of sizes, is dotted here and there on the bookshelves, revealing an interest in travel to far-flung places. The same could be said of the faux zebra skin outlining the sofa (see pages 100–1) and the large-scale antique tiger print above it—an awesome focal point for the room.

Reminders of travel closer to home include the old, rather battered tobacco tin (below) depicting a cowboy and now used to house colored art pencils. The western theme continues on another shelf (see page 98) with

a belt featuring a horse's head that was worn as a child and a belt buckle that sports an obvious love for a country music legend—Hank Williams.

Books are a necessity on bookshelves, but they are certainly not the only things that belong on them. As well as antique globes, we have some wonderful vintage ship artwork. Shelves provide a wonderful opportunity for displaying all sorts of things, such as small pieces of art, sculpture, clocks—whatever has meaning for you.

THE **nautical** influence is undeniable but, with so many other ELEMENTS at *play, not* at all overwhelming

WONDERFUL,
exotic corals and
SHELLS *collected* over time
make a BEAUTIFUL
and *evocative* DISPLAY
on a mantel

Mantels can be tricky things to decorate. Our home has eight fireplaces, and making each one look different takes some serious thought.

As I have said in all my books, I think that a "live" element—and that means live plants—is important to any room. On a grand scale, that could mean a palm tree, which sweeps graciously out from the corner of a room, but on a mantel, a delicate plant in a beautiful, small container fits the bill absolutely perfectly. Antique, leather-bound books make good companions, along with candlesticks, small photographs, and clocks. Continuing the marine theme, petite mirrored frames above this mantel feature bookplates of shells and corals—eye-catching displays against the cobalt-blue wall.

My own business is all about the bedding. Like everything else in the home, it should be tailored to fit the needs of the room, and the room should be tailored to fit the person. A bedroom is a very personal space, where one should be able to relax and feel totally comfortable. As you drift off to sleep, it is important to be surrounded by sights and smells that promote good and peaceful thoughts. In the room above, the familiarity of the blue and white mattress ticking brings instant visual comfort. Piled high with a puffy feather bed and plenty of layers, the comfort becomes physical. The layers of luscious silk velvet and the ticking give off a masculine feel, but that is softened with the modern-style batik, floral pillows, and, of course, white linen.

The mid-century, French-style chest opposite has been reinvented with a silver metallic finish. Hanging in a perfect arrangement on the wall above it, polished chrome frames containing old maps continue the look. While these reflective surfaces keep the setting fresh, the old alabaster lamp grounds it.

In this house lives a kindred spirit, who shares my love of many of the same things. A breathtaking interior has been put together, in particularly artistic ways, with imaginative collections and original vignettes. The eclectic mix of art, collected from travels all over the world, gives the room an especially modern feel.

A gorgeous white piano, with the sculpture carefully balanced on top, acts as the sophisticated anchor of this predominantly white room. Draped in heavy antique chains, the huge pair of antlers hanging over the fireplace—definitely a conversation piece—adds a new level of depth and drama.

You can see that the fireplace is actually used… a lot, but when the weather is warm, a primitive-style bust fills the void. There is nothing quite like a fire to make a room inviting, and it's not just about the heat that it provides—the flickering flames and crackling wood are a seductive invitation to curl up and relax in front of it. Although the books scattered on the mantel above may look randomly placed, they are actually well thought out in terms of color, texture, size, and placement.

Pulling back from the display, one is first mesmerized by the curling animal horns, then the eye is drawn downward to the two small wood and silver boxes, which I adore. They are incredibly versatile, and I like to use them in bookshelves, to stand alone, or in a tabletop display, either to lift another piece higher or to stack one on top of another. Which boxes make the cut? My preference is for antique metal tins that, long ago, were the packaging for some product or other, perhaps tobacco or baking powder. It really doesn't matter. For me, it is all about the graphics, the color, and the patina. Occasionally, I will find a metal box with the brown tortoise look, which is my absolute favorite.

This tabletop collection has been masterfully done, and you can see that its creator knows to put objects of various sizes and heights together—an important point to remember when creating displays yourself. Usually odd numbers work best, but if you are working with pairs, place them at different elevations, for an overall staggered effect. Books are particularly useful for this and make interesting and stable risers.

Even though a display is carefully thought out, it should not appear contrived. It is evident here that this homeowner not only has exquisite taste but has also traveled, amassing a beautifully cultivated collection.

This amazing tabletop collage is a work of art, which is particularly appreciated in a tight shot, as above. You can really appreciate the petite, antique, leather-bound books and the silver pieces and how the two elements have been so expertly used together.

Silver always needs some patina. For me, when it is polished to the point of being bright and shiny, it paradoxically loses some of its luster. The time-worn look has much greater appeal, and the aging books lend themselves to a more subtle shade of silver, too, which is found here in the various collected treasures.

I also like to use silver trays or, as above, the antique silver piece with gorgeous garlands, which shows off the coveted leather books.

Just when I think that my romance with white cannot be outdone, I then come across this room. I love so many interior design styles that it is hard for me to choose a favorite, but this would certainly be a contender.

The Chesterfield sofa is the focal point, but there are so many other amazing elements present that are not to be upstaged. It is all about layers, and I do love layers when decorating. You will notice that it begins with the rug, with deep, rich shades of color, while the dark

paneled walls bring in a warmth. The drapes, made from vintage floral fabrics in the same rich tones, add a touch of femininity to balance the overall heavy masculinity of the room. The horn collection on the wall is quite unique, with each mount from a different period and made up in a very different way. Like all the other wonderful curios and treasures assembled in this space, they have, no doubt, been amassed after a lifetime of travels, to coexist harmoniously and beautifully.

The spectacular array of antique shell boxes shown above, as well as the shells and coral themselves, is a fitting tribute to Mother Nature, and it reveals the homeowner's obvious love of the sea.

The smell of the ocean and the sound of the waves outside your window at night always soothe and promise a good night's sleep. Long-lasting memories are made as you build sandcastles or hunt for the most glorious shells as the sun sets across the water—these are things you never forget. I for one can never resist the quaint little shops on the shore selling shells, boxes made of shells, and ships in a bottle. I love the tinkling of the bell as you walk through the shop door and then seeing items that you normally would never see, unless on a beach vacation. My daughter bought an all-white shell box for me from a store on the beach. It is something that I will always treasure. To surround oneself with memories of the sea is to remind oneself of a life well lived.

CHAPTER 7

A Love of Books

I AM A BOOK LOVER. I GUESS YOU COULD SAY THAT makes me old fashioned, but my kids are the same. We are all tactile and love the feel of a book in our hands as we read. I like to be able to flip through the pages and to breathe in the smell of a book. That sensual experience is something you cannot get from a screen on a handheld device.

I LOVE THE FACT THAT BY READING A BOOK, you can change your life. Books supply knowledge as well as entertain. You can discover how to make a delicious dinner, learn how to decorate a room, or appreciate the words of Shakespeare. The written word is quite amazing and should be cherished, not tossed away into a recycle bin once you have finished.

I happen to have an ongoing romance with design books and magazines. I keep my favorites under my bed, and there is nothing I like more than to lie across it to look at them… one more time.

This bedroom is a sumptuous space, decorated in rich colors and filled with fine furniture (see page 117). Taking center stage is the impressive iron bedstead, with a bookshelf behind that resembles an amazing kind of headboard. The bedding is a French-style toile in a luscious combination of colors and plaids. Most important to me, it is a print that I designed for the New York showroom. I wanted this bedding to be the focal point of the room and I filled in around it with a richly colored rug and, of course, the dramatic velvet drapes that bring it all together.

the RUSTY-COLORED ROSES
are the *perfect* shade for this room,
displayed in one of my
favorite TROPHY CUPS with its
PERFECT *patina*

Adding to the drama of the room is the dark wood Bombay chest, with ornate carvings, positioned next to the bed. I have always wanted a Bombay chest, but they are not that easy to find. I bought this one at an estate sale and quickly moved it into this room to be a part of the mix. Antique books have a practical role to play here, helping to raise the heights of the ornate lampstand and the three-handled trophy cup, which serves as a vase for some gorgeous rusty-colored roses.

bookshelves can become
an *intrinsic* part of a BRILLIANT
DECORATING scheme

Many of the vintage books shown on these pages have extraordinary bindings. Some are gilded, while others are embossed with gorgeous designs. I am always on the look-out for such treasures. A good number of them have already been read, while others have been purchased strictly for their beauty. Stacked together in a pile, with their less-than-perfect covers betraying something of their past history, they make handsome and intriguing statements.

The subject matter of my book collection covers an enormous range, from classic American novels and French treasures to cookbooks, and they are not all vintage and bound in leather. I display all sorts of books, from coffee-table hardbacks to flimsy paperbacks, around the house. The kitchen, for example, is full of all different kinds of cooking and entertaining books, many of which have been passed down from one generation to another.

Bookshelves can become an intrinsic part of a brilliant decorating scheme. Books from a series, such as encyclopedias, in the same size and color, offer a mesmerizing formality lined up neatly on a shelf, while a haphazard collection of paperbacks brings stripes of vivid color to the décor.

Vintage books are like no others. Resting on the floor, next to a piece of furniture, these large French tomes make such a comforting statement. They belong to a series, and are really quite special. Their worn bindings lend a pleasing patina to the room.

Bookshelves should not be reserved just for books. It is important to take advantage of the space they offer to display other favorite things, too, such as old photographs of family members and mementos of sporting triumphs—anything that is meaningful to you.

A masculine antique law book has been reinvented as a display surface for a lamp and a china dog. Helping to raise the dog even higher are two contrasting small boxes, which not only perform a useful strategic role but also look good in their own right.

The charcoal-gray paintwork on one wall of this room arrests the eye completely, drawing it right to the custom-built bookshelves. Bordered by the crisp white trim, the shelves are truly the focal point here. A seating area alongside provides a useful little reading nook.

As well as displaying books of all shapes, colors, and sizes, the shelves are a stage for other treasures. I am always drawn to small vintage oil paintings—there is something so charming about them—and they fit perfectly on top of a stack of books on the bookshelf. I also like to see antique clocks, small lamps, trophy cups, shells, fossils, petite ferns in small urns… The success of any space always comes down to the decorative details.

The light fixture in this room is not to be outdone. As well as looking impressive, this antique chandelier lights the room beautifully. Reflected light is provided courtesy of the large, gilt-edged mirror, which makes the room appear larger. Full-length linen curtains frame the mirror, softening the room and making it even more beautiful. Remember that curtains are not just for windows. Hanging from good-looking rods and finials, they can make anything in a room appear important. This is a great design tip. I even use curtains and rods behind beds as a headboard of sorts, or to border a mirror or a painting that I wish to highlight.

THE CHALKY CHARCOAL-GRAY AND BRILLIANT WHITE PAINTWORK OF THESE SIMPLE BOOKSHELVES FLANKING THE DOORWAY MAKES THEM THE FOCAL POINT OF THE ROOM.

The homeowner was fortunate to inherit this fabulous stash of books. They are now displayed on custom-built bookshelves surrounding the French doors, which open onto a beautiful garden area. The book display is deliberately haphazard, with some books in neat rows and others in jumbled piles. Tarnished trophy cups, antiques, animal horns, and leather-covered antique flasks mingle artfully with the books and other objects of personal interest. Altogether, this is a breathtaking display of how books can really impact an interior.

The French armchair, with its cracked leather and rather battered appearance, matches the time-worn leather on the bindings of the books, which are works of art in themselves. Fitting in nicely with the whole time-worn comfort, of which I am a fan, are the almost threadbare rugs.

the **BINDINGS**
of the **BOOKS** are
works of art
in *themselves*

Warm wood paneling covers every inch of this library space, where one can seek out a quiet place to enjoy reading any of the intriguing titles on the bookshelves. The invitingly furnished room is centered around a stunning stone fireplace, where a crackling fire in the depths of winter makes the space eminently cozy. Again, small paintings and objects of interest are interspersed with the books. Should one prefer to write, rather than read, the delicate secretary is the ideal location.

THE POLISHED WARM TONES OF THE WOOD IN THE LIBRARY ARE REFLECTED IN THE BEAUTIFULLY ARRANGED LEATHER-BOUND BOOKS.

PART THREE

Time to Celebrate

**BARN PARTY CELEBRATION • BRIDAL SHOWER
HAPPILY EVER AFTER**

CHAPTER 8

Barn Party Celebration

NOW I KNOW WHAT YOU ARE ALL THINKING...
HOW COME YOU HAVE A FOURTH OF JULY BARN
party in a book entitled "A Romance with French Living?"
Although I have a passion for French style, I am a native-born
Texan. Like any American, I love my country and I am a great fan
of the red, white, and blue. I have always collected Americana, and here
was my chance to use it. Let's not forget either the tastes that good
ole Southern cooking has to offer.

OUR TOWN has a big Fourth of July parade, and my kids enter a float every year without fail. As for me, I am always involved in its decoration. It all starts with one of our flat-bed trailers. For this year's design, we put a patio table on the trailer, complete with its umbrella draped in red, white, and blue. We then covered the table in a red tablecloth and surrounded it with chairs slipcovered in the patriotic colors. My kids were all similarly dressed, with red, white, and blue beads, hats, and so on. As good as they looked, the cherry on top was the enormous American flags, which came from a school auditorium long ago and which we attached to the front of the trailer by their poles. The sides were draped with antique bunting.

As my son Nick towed the float with his truck down our gravel road to the parade site, he forgot about the trees… or, should I say, he forgot about the clearance needed for the flags, and one of the antique wooden flagpoles was snapped in half. Even so, the float ended up winning a prize for being the most original.

Our barn is huge. It was built in the 1800s from hand-hewn logs of cedar trees growing on the property. I have always dreamed of someday taking the time to clean it up for the ultimate barn party, and that time finally came. My kids were delighted.

Clear party lights were strung from the rafters, while harvest tables were placed end to end and covered in tablecloths and linen drop cloths—yes, the ones that

IN THE PARTY BARN, IT IS ALL ABOUT PATRIOTISM, FROM A CHERISHED VELVET AND CHENILLE FLAG PILLOW TO RED AND BLUE DRINKS. OLD GLORY WAVES PROUDLY FROM THE RAFTERS.

it just would not
be a FOURTH OF JULY
celebration
without WATERMELON

you can buy in the paint department. They are a cheap fix for tablecloths for a casual party. An old dressmaker's mannequin, called Willemina, was set atop the table and draped in flags. An old brass-band horn sat at the base, filled with more flags. We brought out my old Cola Cooler, perfect for keeping red and blue sodas cool— the kids could not wait to pop the tops on these Dublin real-sugar delights! Then there was popcorn—lots of it—which Nick loves. I think he eats it every day of his life... seriously!

An old handmade wooden Uncle Sam presents the chalkboard menu, which displays the food to be served at the party. Naturally, good ole Southern cooking was the feature of the day, with fried chicken, corn on the cob, coleslaw, and, of course, my many kinds of homemade biscuits. My New York photography crew for this book, who are now part of the family, could not wait for the shoot to be over, so that they could chow down on them. I should point out that these are not just any biscuits. I created these combinations myself, all from

scratch. There were sausage and cheese biscuits, which are much like the sausage balls that every Southerner serves. Then I made bacon, cheese, and jalapeno biscuits, and, of course, the basic and delicious Southern buttermilk biscuits. I served them all in the cast-iron skillets they were baked in—my grandmother always insisted that fried chicken and biscuits required a cast-iron skillet. This was a meal that was finger-licking good. After the shoot, we all sat down and thanked God for the food, and for the great nation in which we are honored to live. There is no place on earth like it and we are proud to be Americans... from New York to Texas.

It just would not be a Fourth of July celebration without watermelon. When I was a child, my grandfather showed me the technique for picking the best one. He would have me follow him out into the garden, and we would thump the watermelons, listening for a hollow sound. If it sounds hollow, then it is ripe, was what he told me. He hasn't been wrong yet, as this watermelon was red-ripe, sweet, and delicious.

the hot, buttered
SOUTHERN BISCUITS *tasted*
even *better* than they LOOKED

I have had these vintage firecrackers (above) for years, and I know it may sound a little strange, but the graphics on their wrappers are really works of art. Showing them off under a glass cloche, on top of a vintage reel of ribbon, with my favorite "Singing Sailor" fabric chaircover in the background, is my idea of the perfect layered display.

Our old weathered Uncle Sam (left) is a charming pointer for the chalkboard menu for this Fourth of July party.

FRIED CHICKEN AND NANA'S COLESLAW WERE THE DELICIOUS FOCAL POINTS OF THE PARTY'S SOUTHERN FARE, ALONG WITH MY BISCUITS, OF COURSE.

IT WAS HARD NOT TO EAT THESE HOT BISCUITS WHILE THEY WERE BEING PHOTOGRAPHED, AND THEY TASTED EVEN MORE DELICIOUS THAN THEY LOOKED. ONE OF THE COMBINATIONS WAS INSPIRED BY MY PHOTOGRAPHER'S LOVE OF PEPPERS AND MY LOVE OF SAUSAGE BALLS (SEE RECIPE BELOW).

I HAVE TO ADMIT THAT I DIDN'T MAKE THESE FRUIT OF THE FOREST TARTS—I SPOTTED THEM AT ONE OF MY FAVORITE GOURMET GROCERY STORES IN DALLAS. WITH THOSE COLORS, WHAT COULD BE MORE PERFECT FOR THE FOURTH OF JULY?

Old-fashioned Southern Biscuits

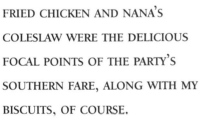

2 cups (250g) unbleached flour

¼ tsp baking soda

1 tbsp baking powder

1 tsp kosher salt

6 tbsp (85g) unsalted butter, plus 2 tbsp (30g) for frying

1 cup (240ml) buttermilk

Makes 12 biscuits

Preheat the oven to 450°F (230°C/gas 8). Combine the dry ingredients in a bowl. Cut the 6 tbsp (85g) butter into chunks, then cut into the flour until it looks like coarse meal. Add buttermilk and combine. If the mix is too sticky, add a bit more flour. If too dry, add a bit more liquid. Flour the work surface and pat out the dough to 1in (25mm) thick—do not roll, pat only, and fold over three times, then give a final pat. Do not overhandle. Cut with a round cutter. Melt the remaining butter in a cast-iron skillet/frying pan. Wipe butter onto the top and bottom of each biscuit as you place it in the pan. Bake for 10–12 minutes until golden.

For Sausage and Cheese Biscuits, add 8oz (250g) chopped cooked sausage and 2 cups (250g) grated Cheddar cheese to the biscuit dough, then pat and cut into rounds.

For Bacon, Jalapeno, and Cheese Biscuits, add 6–8 strips crumbled cooked bacon, 10 chopped pickled jalapeno slices, and 2 cups (250g) grated Cheddar cheese to the biscuit dough and cut into rounds.

CHAPTER 9

Bridal Shower

I COULD NOT BELIEVE IT—MY BABY GIRL WAS GETTING MARRIED! OF COURSE, EVERY GIRL DREAMS of her wedding day, just as every mom dreams of her daughter's wedding. For someone like me, who lives to decorate, it was excitement overload. Alexandria was happy to collaborate, but she wanted me to plan her bridal shower and wedding and relied on me to make them both beautiful. But, like her mother, and grandmother, she is very picky, so I ran everything by her first.

WE KNEW THAT THE WEDDING would be held here at the plantation—Alex had planned that when she was a little girl—and so would her bridal shower. She had already decided that her wedding colors would be aqua and white, but for her shower she opted for girly pink: pink roses, pink punch, and pink food.

I plotted my decorating scheme carefully—after all, it had to be over the top! I designed special slipcovers, the likes of which I had never seen before. I had an overlay of tulle put around the skirt of each chair and filled it with pink rose petals. The guest tables were just as elegant, overlaid with voile and white linen, while the serving tables were skirted in just voile. White fairy lights, draped underneath, twinkled through the sheer fabric. It looked amazing and ethereal. Chandeliers hooked over branches were suspended above the serving tables, which also had a canopy of netting for a romantic feel. The netting had a practical purpose, too, because, when it was pulled around the table, it kept the insects away… brilliant, if I do say so myself.

Like my mother, I have been collecting antique wedding baskets for some time, and between us we have amassed quite a number. Now seemed the perfect time to put them to use, as the base for our flower arrangements. The baskets were filled with all shades of pink roses, pink larkspurs, white stock, and sprigs of baby's breath. I have a great love of flowers and even spent time working at a florist's while I was still in high school. These flowers in their baskets not only looked gorgeous, but also had a scent out of this world.

THE SETTING FOR MY DAUGHTER'S VERY ROMANTIC BRIDAL SHOWER, IN A LUSH GROVE OF OAK TREES THAT PROVIDED THE SHADE, WAS ABSOLUTELY PERFECT.

layering applies
to all sorts of DECORATING,
and that *includes*
BRIDAL SHOWERS

Simple folding chairs in beautiful, frilly, custom-made slipcovers, with pink rose petals inserted into the tulle skirt overlay, are just so romantic, and the white linen and voile tablecloths complement them perfectly. Along with the fabric print lampshades, chandeliers, flowers, and Southern food, this bridal shower became something very special indeed.

I have had this gorgeous white suitcase, with its pink quilted lining, for ever. I always thought that the perfect occasion would present itself when I could show it off, and the moment had finally arrived. With its lid open, it was the perfect adornment on one of the buffet tables, displaying glass containers of candy. I always remember that at every shower I went to when I was growing up,

there were pastel mints and nuts. I know my grandmother would be proud that I carried on the tradition by filling a glass compote with the mints.

An ornate white-framed mirror, hanging from a tree over one of the buffet tables and reflecting the beautiful scene, is inscribed in lipstick—pink, of course—with the words "Alex + Luis," a reminder of the happy event to come.

Ladies and gentlemen, if you still need convincing, this is where I remind you that it is a good thing to collect pretty silver and silver-plate trays, and porcelain and silver cake stands, for occasions such as this. Here, we have stacked cake stands with our lemon and raspberry bars, while trays of all shapes and sizes are piled high with food. See, you're not a hoarder, you're a collector!

The bride's table was made even more special by the lampshades hanging above. We had covered them in various vintage-replica pink prints and then suspended them from the tree branches with antique silk millinery ribbons. Vintage sugar bowls and pitchers decorated with pink roses became the perfect vases for flowers, and my collection of Grande Baroque silverware was put out at every place setting.

Cloth napkins were tied with charming pink ribbons and embellished with a personalized tag dedicated to the shower. These were piled into antique wedding baskets, where each guest could serve themselves.

The food was all homemade by us, and by us, I mean me, my mom, and anyone else who happened to get too near to the kitchen. Alex loves bars of all kinds, so we featured raspberry bars and lemon bars, as well as miniature sugar-free pecan pies. I hate things that taste sugar-free, but with these, no one ever knows that they are not getting the corn-syrup kind of pie.

Alex's favorite cake is coconut, so we knew we would be whipping one up for the bridal shower. It really is delicious and also very easy, which makes it my favorite as well. It was topped with her other favorite… strawberries. I couldn't refuse her, could I? After all, it was her day, although, to be honest, Alex has been something of a princess since she was born, and I love that about her.

No Southern shower would be complete without petits fours and finger sandwiches, either: smoked Gouda pimento cheese, and my mom's famous chicken salad sandwiches and cucumber sandwiches. Yum.

I really did want this to be like a vintage shower—you know, like the showers that those of us who grew up in the South remember. There was always some sort of

CUPCAKES, PETITS FOURS, AND CRUSTLESS SANDWICHES, SHAPED WITH COOKIE CUTTERS, ADORN THE BUFFET TABLE. THE SWAN IS THE QUEEN OF THE BRIDE'S TABLE.

A BREATHTAKING
gathering spot
in *dappled shade*
is made from an OUTDOOR SOFA
laden with *comfy* and gorgeous
PINK PILLOWS

punch at these parties and, like any good Southern mom, I have a beautiful crystal punch bowl and about a million little punch cups. As Alex loves strawberries, we made a delicious strawberry punch.

Alex is obsessed with these pink-striped drinking straws, and I was equally passionate about the vintage containers that housed them and the miniature flower bouquet, so we were both happy.

For the little lounge area that we created, we brought out a pink wool rug and placed a vintage metal lounge seat and an ornate garden table on top. The seat was filled with some of my favorite Carolyn Westbrook Home

pink print pillows, which I had stored away over the years. Now was the perfect occasion to bring them out.

We began weaving our magic the day before the shower. There were no party planners or wedding directors here… I was the ringleader. I leaned over and dangled from tall ladders to hang chandeliers and netting from tree limbs, while Nick dragged over tables, chairs, and the rest of the furniture we needed.

When it was all finished and ready for the big reveal, Alex could not believe her eyes. It was perfect and reflected her taste exactly: dreamy, magical, and sophisticated, and not too glitzy or fake.

CHAPTER TEN

Happily Ever After

THIS IS WHAT WE ALL WISH FOR—THE HAPPILY EVER AFTER... ESPECIALLY FOR OUR CHILDREN. Our families on both sides come from a long line of long marriages. My parents have been married 56 years, Joe's for 58 years, and Joe and I have been married 25 years. As I said, we had always dreamed of a wedding here at The Plantation, since Alexandria was a girl. Now that time was upon us.

my daughter was to have her
fairytale wedding,
and I wanted it to *look like*
A MILLION DOLLARS,
without spending a *million dollars*

Alex wanted a spring wedding. Listen, it really did not matter to me when it took place, I was just so excited to be asked to do all the decoration. I knew my design was going to be over the top—like it wasn't going to be that way anyway, with me involved! I always seem to have to go one step further to make something "just right" and exhaust everyone in the process. I do sometimes wonder whether I might be a creative fanatic, or just a wee bit crazy, or maybe a little bit of both.

My daughter was to have her fairytale wedding, and I wanted it to look like a million dollars, without spending a million dollars. And, if I do say so myself, I think it turned out to be very special indeed.

The wedding ceremony took place on the front lawn beneath an arch that was filled with white flowers of every kind. My friend Sharon, who is a floral arranger, put this magnificent display together with white hydrangeas, white roses, and all sorts of vines, and gorgeous blooms that were quite spectacular. Joe and I were so happy to have my cousin's husband, David, perform the ceremony, as he had married us… a million years ago. The decoration was beautiful.

The tent went up on a nice May day. There had been a number of tornadoes right before, and more storms were predicted, so extra reinforced anchors were needed on the tent, which meant an all-day construction. Of course, this was a family affair, like everything we do around

here, and the troops were gathered, anxiously waiting for the tent people to finish, so we could get started on the important task of decorating. I had sketched off my version of how I thought it would work. I had Plan A, Plan B, and I always have a back-up plan, as I have learned over my years of setting up tradeshows, that you must learn to be the queen of improv, for you never know what can happen.

Against the wedding advisor's best advice, I chose a pole tent, which was less than twice the price of a frame tent and much more dramatic looking. My plan was to decorate the top with swathes of translucent fabric and strings of fairy lights behind, but I had never done anything like it before. To add to the difficulties, there were only two poles to work from and the ceiling was 18 feet (5.5 meters) high. It almost took an acrobat to make this work. After at least five trips to the home improvement store for the correct supplies, many hours later and more than three hundred yards of sheer fabric and thousands of twinkling lights woven throughout the tent, it was done. It was magical to look at.

⟞⟨◦◦◦◦⟩⟞

IN THE UPSTAIRS HALL ONE OF MY FAVORITE FRENCH CHAIRS SITS IN FRONT OF THE WINDOW. ON THIS SPECIAL DAY, ALEXANDRIA'S VEIL AND BOUQUET OF CREAM HYDRANGEAS AND ANTIQUE ROSES ADD TO THE BEAUTY.

I have always heard that it is good luck for it to rain on your wedding day—it did when Joe and I were married, and our marriage has been good so far—but I did hope that the forecast for rain was wrong. Well, the wedding day was upon us but so were the clouds. We crossed our fingers and hoped for the best as we continued to decorate the garden area outside the tent, where we had placed vintage metal outdoor couches for lounging, decked out with white linen and aqua-print pillows. Then the skies let loose and the rain poured down until, five minutes before "go" time, the clouds miraculously parted and the sun started to shine.

As the wedding service began, Joe and I looked at each other, and it all sort of hit us—that our daughter was getting married. Joe looked so handsome in his tux, and it was incredibly touching to watch him as he looped arms with Alex to walk her "down the aisle." The bridesmaids looked beautiful as they descended the stairs, and Carrington, the flower girl, dropped petals for the bride. In no time, the ceremony was over, and everyone moved on to the tent.

The entrance to the tent was defined by French doors, and swags of luscious hop vines were draped from either side and filled with flowers. Alex could not believe her eyes as she stepped into the tent and into an absolute fairytale. The scent of the flowers permeated the air. The champagne was flowing, candles were glowing, and laughter filled the air. Chandeliers hung from the tented ceiling, with the fairy lights twinkling behind.

A wreath of twigs, with sprigs of white orchids slotted through, made a beautiful candelabra, hanging from the ceiling with an aqua silk ribbon. There were white Vendela roses, white stock, glorious white hydrangeas, and baby's breath everywhere you looked.

On one side of the French doors, a beautiful fountain with concrete doves, representing love, spilled out aqua-colored water. I had added a drop of blue food coloring to the water so that it fitted in with the color scheme Alex had chosen. A staggered display of ferns and white hydrangeas at the foot of the fountain added to the desired garden effect. A group of ornate birdcages, filled with white doves, were arranged at different heights on the other side of the French doors, for a layered look.

More roses and lilies were displayed on the mid-century aqua buffet, alongside silver trays, antique candy jars with their contents in the wedding colors, and limeade served in Mason jars. An elaborate mirror behind reflected the tabletop décor.

The tables were draped in the wedding colors of aqua and white, each with a tall, elegant candelabra topped with a ball of cream roses and hydrangeas. With everyone seated, the food was served: Southern pecan chicken, garlic mashed potatoes, French green beans, and a fabulous salad with pecans, feta, grapes, and more. The dessert bar included lemon bars, pecan bars, cheesecake bars, brownies, each one set atop small individual white porcelain cake stands, and, of course, iced tea with mint and lemon and orange slices.

Then there was the wedding cake. It arrived the day before the wedding and I was worried sick about it. It had to be just perfect. I tore into the cake box—carefully—but I need not have worried. The cake looked fantastic. I mean, amazing! It had Tiffany blue icing with

A MID-CENTURY *aqua buffet* is set off by an ELABORATE *mirror*, which *reflects* the TABLETOP décor

gorgeous garlands of flowers swagged around the edge in a pearlized white. We displayed a small tier of cake on a white porcelain cake stand, beneath a glass cloche, with two roses perched on top. At the base of the stand, I added a garland of pale pink roses and white stocks, hydrangeas, and frothy baby's breath.

After the dinner, people gathered in groups, not wanting to leave. It was such a romantic and happy night, with the music playing and the candles twinkling all around. I only realized I had not really got to talk to the bride and groom when they started to leave for their honeymoon. In a convertible Mustang, with a "Just Married" sign fixed to the back, they made their getaway.

As they drove off, Joe and I walked back to the tent and sat there quietly for a while, surveying what we had accomplished. I felt sad that it was all over but I wanted to be able to enjoy the gorgeous setting for just a little longer. My one concern was that Alex had liked it.

At about that time, Nick brought the phone to the tent for me, and it was Alex on the other end. I could not believe it, as she is never one for words. She said, "Thank you, Mom. It was the prettiest wedding that was ever done. I cannot believe that you did all that for us. I love you. Tell Daddy that I love him." I cried. Her words made every bit of all the hard work absolutely worth it. It was "happily ever after" for all.

---

above left and left: THE WEDDING CAKE WAS FANTASTIC! ANTIQUE WEDDING CAKE TOPPERS AND A VINTAGE CARD, SAVED ESPECIALLY FOR THE OCCASION, REPRESENT SOMETHING OLD AND SOMETHING BLUE.

opposite: WITH CANDLES GLOWING, PLACES SET, AND FLOWERS BLOOMING AT EVERY TABLE, THE GORGEOUS AND ROMANTIC WEDDING TENT AWAITS ITS GUESTS.

Index

WEDDING RESOURCES

Thanks to the very talented Rebecca DeJohn whose company, Heaven To Earth, made the beautiful hanging wreaths for the wedding. She is not only an amazing talent, but also an amazing friend, whom I could not do without.

Thanks to my friend Sharon, who made the breathtaking floral archway the couple were married under. She has a fantastic ability to create beauty and has a very successful business, Rose of Sharon, in Sulphur Springs, Texas.

Thanks to Alexander Tent Company located throughout Texas, for the pristine tent and for making sure that it was secured during tornado season. They did a fantastic job.

Thanks to Marsha at Rental Solutions in Kerens, Texas, for providing tips and everything else for the wedding and reception.

Thanks to Francis, who caters everything that we do. She is a fabulous cook and I can always count on her to make us something delicious and beautiful.

Heaven To Earth
Rebecca DeJohn, tel: 903-521-6250
Look for her on Facebook

Rental Solutions
Kerens, Texas
Marsha, tel: 903-654-9272
www.rentalsolutions.com

Alexander Tent Company
Tel: 972-247-8556
www.alexandertent.com

Party Time Catering
Corsicana, Texas
Francis Brazell, tel: 903-874-3387

Rose of Sharon
1978 S. Broadway St.
Sulphur Springs, Texas 75482
Sharon Smith, tel: 903-438-2320

Acknowledgments

Again, i have to thank my wonderful family, as they make everything in my life more beautiful. Thanks to my mother for her constant inspiration, and to my dad for his willingness to help.

To Joe, who is truly my better half and who is always there for me.

To my son Nicholas, who has become such a great man, as he graduates from high school and goes out into the world with a very diverse mix of wonderful skills, from decorating to welding. I know that he will do amazing things.

To my daughter Victoria, who has been blessed with so much creative energy and enthusiasm for life, and the courage to use it.

To Alexandria, my baby who was married to Jose Luis this year. We were able to capture many of those beautiful moments in this book for all to see. I wish you both many, many years of wedded bliss.

To Jose Luis, who fits in perfectly into this crazy family… you are always there when I need help and you can always reach the things that are out of reach.

To Cindy Richards and David Peters, thanks for the opportunity of working together again.

To Gillian Haslam, your expertise, talent, and wonderful personality are always appreciated… thank you.

Thanks, again, to the truly talented team of photographers, Keith Scott Morton and Eric Richards, who I am happy to call my friends. We have worked together in such close quarters over the years and their talent never ceases to amaze me. We have to keep doing books, so that you can continue to come back to Texas for hot peppers and great Mexican food. Love you both!

My friends, clients, and homeowners are always so talented and amazing. They are so kind to let us barge in, to move things around, and to bring in masses of equipment, totally invading their privacy for a day or two. Thanks to all of you for making this book more beautiful.

To Donna Parker, who has a beautiful country property, down in a little town called Roundtop. There were so many beautiful cottages and cabins spread out across the grounds, each one more charming than the last. Thank you for giving us free rein to roam about and take photos of whatever caught our eye, including a vacant house, out in the middle of a field, that we all fell in love with. You have the creative vision not only to save the house, but also to make it a thing of beauty. It takes a passion to take on the houses they say can't be rescued, and that's what makes them the most rewarding. Keep up the good work, my friend.

To Armando and Cinda Palacios, your weekend cottages were a feast for the eyes, and the modern mix in an otherwise country setting was superb. Thank you for letting us in.

To Jacqui Stoneman and Dr. Harry Myers, from the moment I walked in the door, I could see that we were lovers of many of the same unusual things. Your collection of books was amazing and your sense of style and display were masterfully done. You have managed to create an interior that reflects where you have been and your personalities, which is extraordinary. Thank you for sharing your talents.

To Cindy Hanson, thank you for letting us into your Francophile world—it was stunning. I appreciate you allowing us to share your beautiful interior with the world.

To Denise Nixon, thank you for being a client and allowing us into your home and your fabulous backyard oasis. It is a soothing paradise, and one would never know that the city looms just beyond… simply fantastic. It was my pleasure to get to know you and see your creative vision—thank you for that.

To Paige Hull, just off a country road sits your country home that is more urban than country, and full of inspiration. I love your repurposed objects that make for an extraordinary interior, where people want to gather. Congratulations on this beautiful re-do… magnificent job.

To my friend Karen Beach, whose house is a welcoming place for all who enter. I knew Karen through my business, and as she welcomed us into her home, we were reluctant to leave. She can cook like nobody's business and can mix a mean martini, which I greatly appreciated at the end of a long day. Her home is French inspired, especially with her French bulldogs, who add more love to an already warm interior. Thanks for always giving us a place to gather and for sharing your gifts to make this a beautiful book. Much love to you.

To Jacquelyn and Steve, what can I say… you are amazing. You are an inspiration. You are a creative whirlwind of talent, and you are two kind hearts who never see a stray. A house where everyone is welcome, even the random bunnies, the birds, and a couple of rowdy roosters get a beautiful home and plenty of food to eat. Jacquelyn, I love your enthusiasm that never tires, as you move on to the next house or the next project, with more enthusiasm than the first. Thank you Steve for your great friendship and for sharing meals and life… love you both.

Carolyn